We hope you enjoy this book.
Please return or renew it by the due date.
You can renew it at **www.norfolk.gov.uk/libraries**
or by using our free library app. Otherwise you can
phone **0344 800 8020** - please have your library
card and pin ready.
You can sign up for email reminders too.

NORFOLK COUNTY COUNCIL
LIBRARY AND INFORMATION SERVICE

D1465058

Published in Great Britain in MMXVIII by
Book House, an imprint of
The Salariya Book Company Ltd
25 Marlborough Place, Brighton BN1 1UB
www.salariya.com

ISBN: 978-1-912006-99-1

SALARIYA

© The Salariya Book Company Ltd MMXVIII
All rights reserved. No part of this publication may be reproduced, stored in or
introduced into a retrieval system or transmitted in any form, or by any means
(electronic, mechanical, photocopying, recording or otherwise) without the
written permission of the publisher. Any person who does any unauthorised
act in relation to this publication may be liable to criminal prosecution and
civil claims for damages.

1 3 5 7 9 8 6 4 2

A CIP catalogue record for this book is available
from the British Library.

Printed and bound in China.
Printed on paper from sustainable sources.

This book is sold subject to the conditions that it shall not, by way of trade
or otherwise, be lent, resold, hired out, or otherwise circulated without the
publisher's prior consent in any form or binding or cover other than that in
which it is published and without similar condition being imposed on the
subsequent purchaser.

Created and designed by
David Salariya.

Visit
www.salariya.com
for our online catalogue and
free fun stuff.

PAPER FROM

SUSTAINABLE
FORESTS

Author:
John Townsend worked as a
secondary school teacher before
becoming a full-time writer.
He specialises in illuminating and
humorous information books for
all ages.

Artist:
David Antram studied at
Eastbourne College of Art and then
worked in advertising for 15 years
before becoming a full-time artist.
He has illustrated many children's
non-fiction books.

Truly Foul & Cheesy™
Disasters
Facts &
Jokes

This Truly Foul & Cheesy
book belongs to:

....

Written by
John Townsend

Illustrated by
David Antram

BOOK HOUSE
a SALARIYA imprint

Introduction

Warning – reading this book might not make you **LOL** (laugh out loud) but it could make you **GOL** (groan out loud), feel sick out loud or **SEL** (scream even louder). If you are reading this in a library by a **SILENCE** sign... get ready to be thrown out!

Disclaimer: The author really hasn't made anything up in this book (apart from some daft limericks and jokes). He checked out the foul facts as best he could and even double-checked the fouler bits to make sure – so please don't get too upset if you find out something different or meet a world expert, total genius or a disaster boffin who happens to know better.

If I had my way, I'd RATify the lot!'

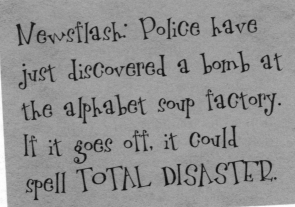

Newsflash: Police have just discovered a bomb at the alphabet soup factory. If it goes off, it could spell TOTAL DISASTER.

Official warning

This book contains some of the weirdest, daftest and foulest mess-ups, muddles and mayhem; from going pear-shaped and belly-up to large-scale disasters. Yes, this is a fantastic farrago of failure.

We all make mistakes, of course (some more than others) and things go wrong all the time. You can always bet that if something can go wobbly IT WILL... but some of the blunders, bloopers and bloomers in this book are BIG TIME.

This is a crazy catalogue of eye-watering accidents, gaffs and botch-ups; from clumsiest clangers and craziest crashes to funniest flops, mind-boggling mix-ups and silliest slip-ups. If you're a bit squeamish or easily disgusted... look away now!

If you ask me, this book is a total disaster!

Disasters

All through history there have been the most appalling tragedies and losses of life due to accidents, wars and natural disasters. Only some can be mentioned here and it is certainly not the intention to make light of tragic events.

In fact, we often use the term 'that was a disaster' when it was only something 'a bit bad'. The dictionary describes a disaster as a sudden accident or a natural catastrophe that causes great damage or loss of life.

But there are also personal disasters on a smaller scale like 'an event or fact that has unfortunate consequences.' Some of those can make us laugh – just like all those video clips on TV showing people falling into swimming pools or crashing into fences on skateboards. Comedy and tragedy often go side by side. Sometimes there's only a whisker between the comic and tragic.

Disastrous Limerick

The circus was such a disaster
When the clumsiest crazy
ringmaster
Swung from the trapeze
And fell to his knees...
SPLAT! He needed a very
big plaster!

While on the subject of circuses...

No wonder many circuses closed down in the 20th century. Before health and safety laws, public entertainment could be very risky. Many travelling circuses met disastrous ends.

Dangerous entertainment has often ended in failure or worse. The trapeze is one of the most dangerous circus acts and, even when carefully rehearsed, nothing can prevent an act going horribly wrong due to mechanical failure. In 1872, Fred Lazelle and Billy Millson, two famous trapeze artists, crashed to the ground in front of a gasping crowd. The trapeze mechanism failed and another gymnast was under the trapeze when it fell. All three men were injured but the circus still had to go on. That's show business!

In the same year, another circus horror made the newspapers when a one-armed lion-tamer in Bolton, UK was mauled to death by lions in front of hundreds of people. Thomas Maccarte, known as Massarti, was attacked by a lion called Tyrant, then three other lions quickly joined in. So, next time someone moans that a show was 'a bit of a calamity', it's worth remembering that some shows really have ended in disaster.

Yum - juicy ringmaster with a whipped topping.

Lion-tamer joke

A woman told the ringmaster she wanted to join the circus as a lion-tamer. The ringmaster asked if she had any experience. 'Why, yes. My father was one of the most famous lion-tamers in the world, and he taught me everything he knew,' she said proudly.

'Really?' said the ringmaster. 'Did he teach you how to make a lion jump through a flaming hoop?'

'Yes, he did,' she replied.

'And did he teach you how to make six lions form a pyramid and roar to command?'

'Yes, he did.'

'And have you ever stuck your head in a lion's mouth?'

'Just the once,' she answered with a worried look. The ringmaster asked, 'Why only once?' She paused and whispered, 'I was looking for my father.'

Silly Circus jokes

Did you hear about the disastrous circus fire in the big top? The heat from the flames was 'in tents'.

Did you hear about the one-legged clown who had to leave the cheesy circus? Alas, he couldn't get his stilton.

Did you hear about the factory that makes clown shoes? It's taken huge steps to avoid a tumble – which is no small feat.

14

Circus tiger

A father and his small son were standing in front of the tiger's cage at the circus. Father was explaining how ferocious and strong tigers are and what a disaster it would be if the tiger escaped. His son thought for a while and said, 'Daddy, if the tiger got out of his cage and ate you up ...'

'Yes, son?' the father said expectantly. The boy continued, 'I would call that a real disaster.' His father patted his head and smiled proudly. 'That's my boy.'

'After all,' his son went on, 'I haven't got a clue what bus I should take to get home.'

Roarrr!

15

Our circus act is a real show-stopper.

Roman Circus

In AD 27 in the town of Fidenae near Rome, a local businessman built a massive wooden amphitheatre on the cheap to stage gladiatorial games (the sort where criminals were executed and people were torn apart by lions for entertainment). During the opening ceremony, the whole structure collapsed, killing 20,000 bloodthirsty spectators and injuring many more (as well as lions). This is by far the worst stadium disaster in history.

Floods

You don't want to know this...

When foul, filthy, stinking water and sludge floods homes, the effects are disastrous enough. But sometimes floods can bring far more than water into houses.

I only wanted a quick bite - but this is ridiculous!

In the Australian floods of 2011, a shopkeeper in Queensland was terrified to see a 2-metre long bull shark swimming around a McDonald's takeaway – 12 miles inland from the sea. The man had to hide waist-deep in floodwater inside his shop for two hours while the shark swam outside looking for prey. Bull sharks are known to attack people and they can survive in salt and freshwater. They are common all over Australia – even indoors when floodwaters rise. So be careful if the kitchen floods... a shark could be hiding in the fridge.

I'm not gill-ty. These jokes are wearing a bit fin.

Limerick

As you sneak to the fridge
in the dark,
Look out for a passing bull shark...
If the flood waters rise,
It's a disastrous surprise...
'I'm dinner!' is your final remark.

Fouler Floods

Most of the floods that make the news are due to a deluge of water. But some are more unusual than that.

In 1814, a 7-metre-high vat of beer on the roof of a brewery in London began to crack. One of the metal hoops around the huge container suddenly snapped, spewing out beer with such force that it knocked into the other vats on the rooftop, and they all burst too. The chain reaction sent nearly 325,000 gallons of beer (1,224,00 litres) cascading off the roof.

The beer flooded the streets of the crowded slum below, demolishing two nearby houses. People grabbed containers and scooped up the beer for a free drink and in all the chaos, eight people drowned. Another person died days later from alcohol poisoning. Death by beer must have been brew-tal.

Death by treacle

In 1919, a tank holding 2.5 million gallons (over 11 million litres) of sticky black treacle (molasses), suddenly burst in Boston, USA. A wave of syrupy liquid rushed through the streets at about 35 mph (56 km/h), killing 21 people and injuring about 150.

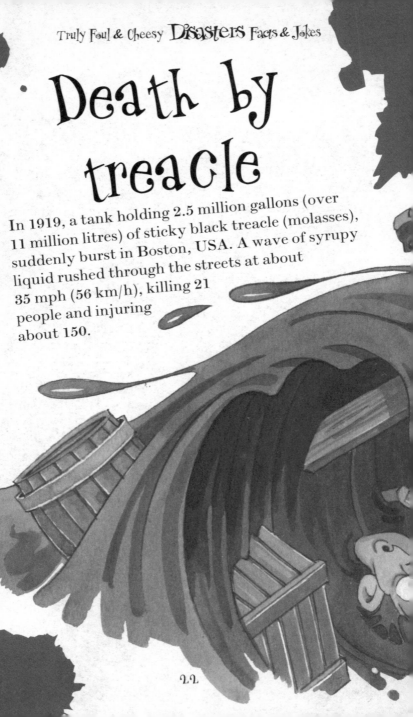

The streets of Boston's North End neighbourhood were swamped with the gooey mess, which knocked over a train and carried along barrels and boxes as it covered two city blocks. This terrible event has entered local folklore and for decades afterwards, residents claimed on hot summer days the area still smelt of treacle.

Whoops!

JOKES

(when floods get serious)

It was raining so much today; the sparrows were piling sandbags round their nests. Even the ducks were wearing lifejackets and a blue whale was seen queuing in McDonalds for Mckrill.

When rising sea levels flooded New Orleans, the Federal Emergency Management Agency declared Louisiana a state of emergent sea. (Emergency!)

It was a terrible storm and the heavy rain didn't stop for days. Soon the entire town was flooded. In a house near the river, eight-year-old Jimmy sat at the window of his upstairs room and stared outside. He watched a sunhat floating where the front lawn used to be. It drifted in one direction for a while, then floated back towards the house. This went on for hours – the hat swirling up and down and back again.

When Jimmy's uncle came by in a rowing boat to see if all was well, he asked Jimmy what he was staring at down there. He saw the hat moving up and back, up and back and asked, 'What's going on down there?'

Jimmy shrugged, 'That's Pa. Last week he said, 'I'm going to mow the lawn on Saturday come hell or high water!''

GURGLE

25

Major Disasters

China has experienced some of the worst disasters on record, if measured by the number of people killed or injured. Two of the three catastrophic Chinese events in history were floods and the first was a devastating earthquake.

Shaanxi Earthquake

In 1556, the deadliest earthquake ever recorded occurred in the Shaanxi province in northern China. At least 830,000 people were killed. This staggering death toll is believed to have reduced the population of the region by 60 percent.

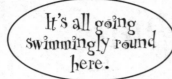

Yellow River Flood

One of the worst floods in human history and the second deadliest disaster ever, occurred in 1887. The Yellow River burst its banks in China's Henan Province. The flood devastated 11 large Chinese towns and hundreds of villages, leaving millions homeless. The flood waters covered 50,000 square miles, killing about 900,000 to 2,000,000 people.

Central China Floods

The worst natural disaster in history, the Central China Floods, occurred in 1931, when the Yangtze River overflowed on a huge scale. Probably 3.7 million people died from drowning, disease and starvation. It is thought that more than 51 million people, or one quarter of China's population, were affected by the devastating Central China Floods.

Shipping disasters

The sinking of the Titanic is probably the most famous shipping disaster of all time. On 15th April 1912, the most luxurious 'unsinkable' ocean liner ever built sank on its maiden voyage. Over 1,500 people lost their lives when the ship ran into an iceberg and soon went down below the icy waves. The ship had too few lifeboats for all the passengers. Many of the women and children (and two dogs) managed to escape into the freezing night on lifeboats. The captain, standing on the bridge, went down with his ship.

AAAAAAAAAAHHHH!

TITANIC

It's so annoying when that happens.

One theory about the sinking of the Titanic is that the lookout in charge watching for icebergs didn't have a pair of binoculars. He was Fred Fleet, one of the few crew members to survive. He was the first to spot the iceberg, and he later said that, if he'd had binoculars, he might have seen it soon enough to give a warning to avoid it. The ship would never have sunk and the dreaded disaster would have been prevented.

Tonight will go down in history.

Let's hope this lifeboat doesn't.

Let me take your drinks order Anyone for ice?

However, it seems the binoculars were on board all along. They were locked up, and the key to the locker wasn't on board. That's because the night before the Titanic sailed, the company running the cruise decided to replace the ship's second officer. As he waved goodbye to the departing Titanic, David Blair (the officer who'd been replaced) didn't realise the locker keys were still in his pocket. Oops.

Ballad of the lost liner

The Captain stood where a captain should
As Titanic sank right down...
Below those waves to the watery graves
Where the brave and lonely drown.

Some crewmen fled from the sinking dead
By making their escape,
So jumped the queue to lifeboats few,
Unready and un-shipshape.

They rowed and rowed, their pace not slowed,
Through waves the tillers steered.
What bleak hours passed, until at last
A rescue ship appeared (The Carpathia)

Once hauled aboard, with their hope restored,
Survivors cast their eyes
Over empty seas in the icy breeze
Where still The Titanic lies.

The wind still blows over sea ice-floes
And the deathly bleak sunrise,
As the grey waves roll with each lost soul...
Where still The Titanic lies.

If only...

33

Five and a half years after the Titanic disaster, another major shipping tragedy struck North America. It was the end of 1917 and World War I still raged in Europe. The port city of Halifax in Canada was busy with ships carrying troops, supplies and ammunition across the Atlantic ocean.

On the morning of 6th December, a French cargo ship called Mont Blanc carrying high explosives collided with the Norwegian vessel Imo. Spectators gathered along the waterfront to see the Mont Blanc on fire, as it brushed by a pier, setting it ablaze.

34

You can tell when things are really bad – it's like rats leaving a sinking ship.

The Halifax Fire Department responded quickly but the Mont Blanc suddenly exploded in the largest explosion of all time (until the first atomic bomb in WW2). More than 1,800 people were killed and 9,000 injured. Almost the entire north end of the city of Halifax, including over 1,600 homes, was flattened. The resulting shock wave shattered windows 50 miles away, and the sound of the explosion could be heard hundreds of miles away. This was the most devastating manmade explosion in the pre-atomic age.

Shipwreck joke

Despite the many appalling disasters at sea through history, there are still cheesy jokes about being shipwrecked to help us cope with the unthinkable (but not the unsinkable).

During a terrible storm at sea, a huge tanker ship, with its cargo of blue and red paint starts to sink. Despite pumping much of the paint from the tanks, the ship breaks up and the captain jumps overboard. A day later he wakes up on a deserted island. He can't believe what he sees. The sand is a strange purple colour. He walks around the purple island to see purple grass, purple birds and purple crabs in purple rock pools. He's shocked when he finds that his skin is purple too. 'Oh no!' he cries, 'I've been marooned!'

Date	Location	Deaths	Magnitude	Effects
January 23, 1556	China, Shansi	830,000	~8	Damage up to 270 miles away
July 27, 1976	China, Tangshan	255,000 (official) 655,000 (estimated)	7.5	Estimated death toll as high as 655,000.
Dec. 26, 2004	Sumatra, Indonesia	228,000+	9.1	Deaths from earthquake and tsunami
August 9, 1138	Syria, Aleppo	230,000	n/a	
Jan. 12, 2010	Haiti	222,570	7.0	1.3 people million displaced.
May 22, 1927	China, near Xining	200,000	7.9	Large fractures.

Natural Disasters

Our planet can be a dangerous place. Violent weather is bad enough but it's not just scary things falling from the sky we must worry about. There are dangers under our feet, too...

According to my calculations... get ready to SCREAM!

SHAKE!

The Earth's crust is moving and shaking all the time but sometimes a massive quake can have devastating effects. Here are the 6 most disastrous earthquakes of all time, based on the number of human casualties (according to Live Science). Death statistics are estimates, as many people die from earthquake after-effects such as fires, flooding and disease.

Did you know?

The earthquake that caused the infamous Indian Ocean tsunami of 2004 was said to have the energy of 23,000 atomic bombs. According to some scientists, the energy released was so great, the Earth's rotation was slightly altered and wobbling of its axis occurred by 2.3 cm. The giant wave that was caused reached 14 countries and in places reached 50 metres high.

Can you believe it?

After Haiti's massive earthquake in 2010, Evans Monsignac lay trapped in the rubble for a whole month before he was rescued. Weak, starving and injured, Evans was described as a living miracle when he was finally dug from the ruins after an extraordinary 27 days trapped in the debris. This is believed to be the longest anyone has survived such an ordeal. Evans was the last person found alive after the earthquake levelled Port-au-Prince to the ground.

He said that he survived by sipping sewage that oozed underneath the rubble of the marketplace where he was buried, a place where sanitation was lacking even before the earthquake. 'It was trickling past where I was lying,' he said. As he recovered in hospital, Evans went on to say, 'Now I know that I must live life to the best I can each day.'

Earthquake riddles

Q: What do cows produce during an earthquake?
A: Milkshake

Q: What happens when a building falls down in San Francisco?
A: Everyone know it's San Andreas' Fault.

Cheesy Newsflash

A massive earthquake in Japan is having a serious knock-on effect for that country's banking industry. Origami bank has folded. Sumo bank has gone belly up. Bonsai bank has cut back some of its branches. Karaoke bank has been put up for sale and is going for a song. Analysts report that there is something fishy going on at Sushi Bank and staff there fear they may get a raw deal. Meanwhile, shares in Kamikaze Bank have nose-dived and 500 jobs at Karate Bank will be chopped.

Volcanoes

Erupting volcanoes can be devastating and have killed millions of people through history. Even so, piles of volcanic ash can be useful in adding nutrients to soils, creating perfect conditions for many crops. Here are five of the deadliest volcanoes of all time:

All I said was, 'I lava you' – and now this...

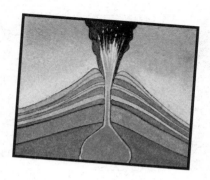

1 Mount Vesuvius

In Italy in AD 79, this Italian volcano devastated the nearby cities of Pompeii and Herculaneum. Thousands of people are thought to have died and the remains of many were preserved by the ash and today look like statues. Since then, Vesuvius has erupted several times, most recently in 1944. It may well erupt again.

2 Mount Ruiz

Mount Ruiz in Columbia, South America, had two major eruptions in 1985. A mixture of mud, ash, and water raced down the volcano's slope and buried a town 30 miles from the volcano, killing around 25,000 people.

3 Mount Pelée

The worst volcanic disaster of the 20th century was the eruption of Mount Pelée in 1902. This was on the island of Martinique in the Caribbean and it killed around 30,000 people. Before the eruption, tremors and gas disturbed many deadly snakes, which wriggled down from the mountains. They killed about 200 animals and 50 people before the exploding volcano killed nearly everyone else.

If the snakes get us, we'll be hisssstory!

Mount Krakatoa

In 1883, Indonesia's volcano Krakatoa exploded, killing over 35,000 people mainly due to resulting tsunamis (huge ocean waves). The biggest explosion was heard more than 2,000 miles away in Australia.

5 Mount Tambora

This is one of Indonesia's 100-plus active volcanoes. Its eruptions in 1815 rocked the world with disastrous after-effects. It caused disease and harmed climate and crops as far away as North America, where heavy snow fell all through the summer. The huge ash cloud blotted out sunlight for months, after its explosions killed over 90,000 people.

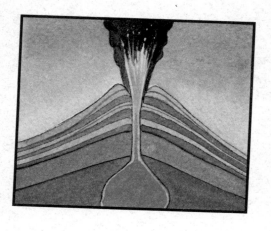

But the worst volcanic nightmare could still be to come...

In the state of Wyoming in the USA there's a 'super-volcano' under Yellowstone National Park. It is thought that it last erupted about 600,000 to 700,000 years ago, and some scientists think there may be another eruption there again one day. If it did erupt again, it could kill billions of people and devastate continents. That could be the disaster of all disasters. There again, it may never happen at all. So, take a deep breath and read on...

3 SILLY
VOLCANIC RIDDLES

Q: Apart from being dangerous, why are some volcanoes so funny?
A: Because they're in the mountains and hill areas (hilarious).

Q: How do we know very old volcanoes used to smell very bad?
A: Because they are ex-stinked (extinct).

Q: What do you call a sleeping volcano?
A: Don't call it anything… best keep quiet in case you wake it up! (Yes, it's dormant.)

Deadliest storms

Storms in the Bay of Bengal account for seven of the ten deadliest hurricanes, typhoons and cyclones in recorded history. These are the top five:

 **1970 Bhola cyclone,**

Bangladesh (East Pakistan).
Death toll 150,000 to 550,000.

 **1737 Hooghly River cyclone,**

India and Bangladesh.
Death toll: 350,000.

3 1881 Haiphong typhoon,
Vietnam.
Death toll: 300,000.

4 1839 Coringa cyclone,
India.
Death toll: 300,000.

5

1584
Backerganj
cyclone,

Bangladesh.
Death toll: 200,000.

Giant hailstones each weighing 1kg fell from the sky in the Gopalganj district of Bangladesh in 1986. The ice balls were the biggest on record, killing 92 people who were unable to escape.

Although 'severe weather events' continue to batter our planet, we're getting better at forecasting them and being prepared than in the past when they struck without warning. However, you can never be prepared for the 5 cheesiest severe weather riddles on the planet…

MOooooooooo

Q: Whatever happened to the cow that was lifted into the air by the tornado?
A: It was an udder disaster.

Q: What's the difference between a horse and wet weather?
A: One is reined up while the other rains down.

Q: What does a cloud wear under its raincoat?
A: Thunderwear.

Q: What's the difference between weather and climate?
A: You can't weather a tree, but you can climate (climb it).

Q: What do you call it when it rains chickens and ducks?
A: Foul (fowl) weather.

Deadly disease

Throughout history there have been some scary epidemics of infectious diseases. Two of the worst pandemics (that's an outbreak that spreads across a whole country, continent or the world) were:

Plague

The bubonic plague or 'Black Death' killed almost 33 percent of the entire population of Europe when it struck between 1347 and 1350. It also affected millions in Asia and North Africa. Killer bacteria were spread due to filthy conditions, poor hygiene and fleas carried by rats.

At least 75 million people are believed to have perished throughout this pandemic, with some estimates as high as 200 million. The plague's name comes from the black skin spots on the sailors who brought the disease from Asia.

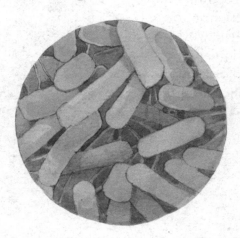

Influenza

In 1918 and 1919, a severe outbreak of flu struck across the world, causing up to 75 million deaths (or possibly killing nearer 100 million people). In India alone, there were over 16 million deaths. This viral disease spread quickly, especially in the close living quarters of all the troops fighting in World War I. They then carried it worldwide when returning home at the end of 1918.

Known as 'Spanish Flu', this pandemic struck about one-third of the world population and killed 20 percent of those who caught it.

Disastrous fancy dress

A French Foul Fact of the Fourteenth Century (try saying that very fast a few times!)

In 1393, King Charles VI of France hosted a ball and had the brilliant idea of dressing up with five of his friends as savages. That meant covering themselves with oily pitch and feathers (pitch was used as fuel for flame torches then).

The men entered the ball chained together in the dark, so someone approached with a torch to get a better look. Big mistake. The men instantly went up in flames. The king was saved by a woman throwing her petticoats over him to put out the blaze. One of his blazing friends threw himself into a vat of water.

The other victims of this bizarre accident weren't so lucky. Two burned alive that night at the ball. The other two died within days from their injuries. The moral of the story is; only to go to fancy dress parties in fireproof clothes and never as a flammable savage.

Madame, I've just barbecued your bloomers!

A dozen dangerously disastrous puns

1 A man sued an airline company after it failed to find his luggage after a crash. Sadly, he lost his case.

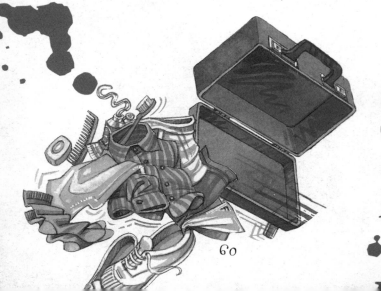

I'm speechless – in fact, totally disGRUNTled.

2 If a wild pig kills you, does it mean you've been boared to death?

3 Have you heard about the fire in the shoe factory? Hundreds of soles were lost.

4 Coffee is the silent victim in our house. It gets mugged every day.

5 My teacher told me my spellings were a disaster so I said I didn't think it was a big deal that I can't spell 'Armageddon'. It's not like it's the end of the world.

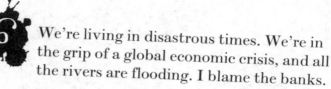

6 We're living in disastrous times. We're in the grip of a global economic crisis, and all the rivers are flooding. I blame the banks.

7 What a disaster! I went into the kitchen and found my fridge had exploded. I think the sausages must have gone off. Then I injured my finger preparing cheese for the pasta. So now I have grater problems. As if that wasn't disastrous enough, when I was chopping up carrots into little cubes, the Grim Reaper appeared right beside me. In that instant, I knew I was dicing with death.

You need a rest - you look like death.

8 Tragically, a famous scrabble champion was found dead on a campsite in a tent, with the tiles, A, E, I, O and U scattered over the body. Police suspect vowel play. It might be murder or assault within tent.

I can't tell any jokes as I'm a little hoarse.

9 My friend's horse fell over and hurt its leg, so the vet told her to keep it indoors all the time. It's now completely stable. The trouble is, the horse likes to come out only when it gets dark, which is a real night mare.

10 I had a fun childhood as we didn't have a bathroom or washing machine. My mum would dunk us in the river, then my dad would put us inside tyres and roll us downhill to spin us dry. They were Goodyears.

Since I became a vegetarian, my life has been full of missed-steaks.

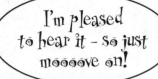

I'm pleased to hear it - so just mooooove on!

 I was nearly killed by a man in the street throwing milk and cheese at me. I thought, 'how dairy!'

 Why did the librarian slip and fall on the library floor under the 'Disasters' shelf? She was in the non-friction section.

Top 6 MOST EXPENSIVE accidents of all time

Insurance policies are like hospital gowns - they never quite cover everything.

Exxon Valdez
– $2.5 Billion

The huge oil tanker Exxon Valdez carried enough sticky, smelly crude oil to fill 125 Olympic-sized swimming pools. One night in March 1989, it hit underwater rocks off Alaska. By morning the ocean had turned black and the air was thick with the stench of oil. Dead fish, seabirds, otters and other wildlife littered the shore.

Why? The ship's captain, Joseph Hazelwood, had left the controls and the ship crashed into a reef, spewing 10.8 million gallons of oil into the beautiful Prince William Sound (accessible only by helicopter and boat). Cleaning up this environmental disaster was one of the costliest accidents of the 20th century, although you are about to discover the most expensive of all. Can you guess what it was and the cost?

Piper Alpha Oil Rig
- $3.4 Billion

The Piper Alpha platform in the North Sea was the world's single largest oil producer, producing 317,000 barrels of oil per day. It became better known as the world's worst off-shore oil disaster.

On 6th July, 1988, technicians removed and checked safety valves as part of normal maintenance. There were 100 identical safety valves which were checked but unfortunately, the technicians made a mistake and forgot to replace one of them.

That night, a technician pressed a start button for the liquid gas pumps and the world's most expensive oil rig accident was triggered. Within 2 hours, the 100-metre platform was engulfed in flames. It eventually collapsed, killing 167 workers and resulting in $3.4 billion in damages.

PLOP!

69

Challenger Explosion
– $5.5 Billion

The American shuttle orbiter Challenger broke up 73 seconds after lift-off, bringing a devastating end to the spacecraft's 10th mission. On 28th January, 1986 the disaster claimed the lives of all seven astronauts aboard. A faulty seal leaked gas which ignited and caused a massive explosion. The whole event was seen by millions on live TV around the world.

The cost of replacing the Space Shuttle was $2 billion in 1986 ($4.5 billion in today's dollars). The cost of investigation, problem correction, and replacement of lost equipment cost $450 million from 1986-1987 ($1 billion in today's dollars).

Prestige Oil Spill – $12 Billion

On 13th November, 2002, the Prestige oil tanker was carrying 77,000 tons of heavy fuel oil when one of its twelve tanks burst during a storm off Galicia, Spain. Fearing that the ship would sink, the captain called for help but the authorities refused to allow the leaking ship close to shore. The storm eventually split the tanker in half and released 20 million gallons (90 million litres) of oil into the sea. One estimate put the total clean-up operation at a staggering $12 billion.

Space Shuttle Columbia
– $13 Billion

On 1st February, 2003, the space shuttle Columbia broke apart while re-entering the atmosphere over Texas, killing all seven crew members on board.

Houston, we've got a problem.

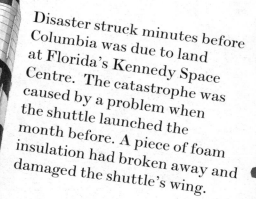

Disaster struck minutes before Columbia was due to land at Florida's Kennedy Space Centre. The catastrophe was caused by a problem when the shuttle launched the month before. A piece of foam insulation had broken away and damaged the shuttle's wing.

Finding out exactly what went wrong became the costliest aircraft accident investigation in history. The search and recovery of debris alone cost $300 million. The final cost of the accident came to about $13 billion.

Chernobyl – $200 Billion

BANG

26th April, 1986, was the date of the costliest accident in history. The world's worst nuclear accident happened at the Chernobyl nuclear plant near Kiev in Ukraine. Experts believe that thousands of people died and as many as 70,000 suffered severe poisoning.

If that wasn't bad enough, a large area of land may still be contaminated for the next 150 years. The 18-mile radius around Chernobyl was home to almost 150,000 people who all had to be evacuated forever. 1.7 million people were directly affected by the disaster.

However could such a devastating disaster be allowed to happen? It all started when workers at the plant were testing the system and shut off the emergency safety cooling mechanism. Even when warning signs of dangerous overheating showed, no one thought to stop the test. Gases built up and at 1:23 a.m. the first explosion rocked the reactor. A total of three explosions eventually blew the 1,000-ton steel top right off. A huge fireball erupted into the sky. Flames shot 1,000 feet into the air for two days, as the entire reactor began to melt down. Radioactive material was thrown into the air like fireworks.

In the eventual clean-up operation, many workers (maybe 4,000) died from radiation poisoning. Thyroid cancer has increased tenfold in Ukraine since the accident. The entire 1986 disaster cost over £200 billion in clean-up and in the value of lost farmland but the loss to lives and people's futures can never be measured. We can only hope that important lessons have been learned.

Random horrors from last century

Terror from the sky

Just after 7 a.m. on 30th June, 1908, a blinding light flashed across the sky in Siberia, followed by a massive explosion over the Tunguska River. The shock wave from whatever exploded has since been estimated to have been hundreds of times more powerful than the first atom bomb. It destroyed a vast area of forest and knocked people off their feet more than 40 miles away.

Amazingly, no one was killed in the explosion, but its effects were felt across the world. Skies were so bright that people in Asia could read newspapers outdoors at night. Experts thought a meteor strike was to blame, but when Russian scientists studied the remote blast site years later, they found no sign of an impact crater.

One explanation was that an icy comet hit the Earth and evaporated on impact, leaving no evidence of itself behind. Probably more likely is that a huge meteor exploded in the upper atmosphere and broke into tiny pieces, slamming shock waves into the Tunguska Forest. Fortunately, it didn't explode over a city.

Deadly Smog

Smog is a dangerous mix of dense fog and deadly fumes such as sooty black coal smoke. Such air pollution used to affect many cities before 'clean air' laws were introduced.

Londoners suffered a bad killer smog in the winter of 1952, when 12,000 people died in four days. A sudden cold snap mixed with the city's chimney smoke, causing dense smoky fog to build up. It wasn't even possible to see your own hand stretched out in front of your face!

Thousands of people and animals were affected by 'black lung', making it hard to breathe, before the deadly smog finally swept out to sea. London has worked on cleaning up its air ever since.

City life isn't just dangerous - it's a rat race.

Elephant Rampage

Most ghastly events are totally unpredictable. If we knew they were coming, we could be prepared and avoid them. They often come suddenly out of the blue – or even out of the jungle.

In 1972, a herd of elephants was driven to madness by extremely high temperatures and no water to drink anywhere. India's Chandaka Forest, already scorched by drought, was hit by a terrible heat wave. By mid-summer the local elephants, normally fairly calm and no threat to humans, all went berserk and stampeded through five villages. They flattened everything in their path and trampled anyone in their way, leaving 24 people dead.

Poisonous Gas Cloud

In August, 1986, in a valley in north Cameroon in Africa, around 1,700 people and 3,500 animals suddenly dropped dead for no apparent reason.

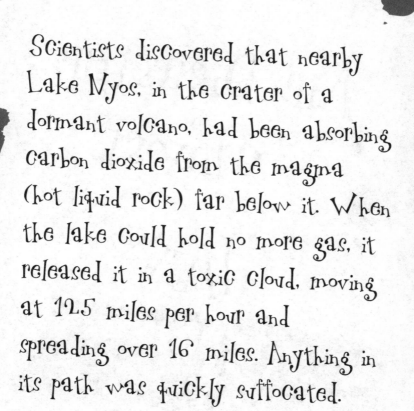

Scientists discovered that nearby Lake Nyos, in the crater of a dormant volcano, had been absorbing carbon dioxide from the magma (hot liquid rock) far below it. When the lake could hold no more gas, it released it in a toxic cloud, moving at 12.5 miles per hour and spreading over 16 miles. Anything in its path was quickly suffocated.

Deadly gas seeping up from the ground in volcanic areas has choked thousands of people in different areas over the years.

Air Disaster...
almost

HEELLLPP!

It seems there have been just as many near-disasters as actual disasters. Although air crashes are now quite rare, there have been some scary near misses.

In 1990, on a flight from Birmingham to Malaga, a large chunk of windshield from a British Airways aircraft fell off the plane. The pilot was instantly sucked from the cockpit and pulled out through the gap. A steward in the cockpit was able to grab his legs just in time. The captain remained dangling out of the gap for 15 minutes and miraculously only suffered frostbite and a few fractures.

The cause of the nearly disastrous British Airways Flight 5390 was found to be the wrong bolts used to replace the windshield just two days before the accident. What a blunder!

DEADLY
disastrous
jokes and puns

I heard a story that a bank robber threw a stick of dynamite right across the street into the bank vault but a dog chased it, picked it up and brought it all the way back to him. BOOM! It all sounds a bit far-fetched to me.

These jokes are cheesier than a mousetrap.

Breaking News: A disaster at the cheese factory. The whole lot exploded. There's nothing left but a pile de Brie! (debris)

Newsflash: A small plane crashed into the big wheel at the funfair. The pilot is stuck at the top and is in a coma but he's gradually coming round.

I accidentally swallowed some food colouring the other day. The doctor says I'll be fine, but I feel like I've already dyed a little inside.

These jokes are killing me.

An old man was very ill in hospital and his son went to visit him. Suddenly, the father began to breathe heavily and grabbed the pen and pad by the bed. With his last gasp, he wrote a note, dropped it, and died.

The son was so overcome with grief that he didn't remember slipping the note into his pocket. At the funeral, he reached into the pocket of his coat and immediately felt the note. He excitedly read it thinking it might be something he could recite during the service. It said: **YOU IDIOT – GET OFF MY OXYGEN TUBE!**

Did you see that documentary on the history of the pick-axe for gravedigging? It was ground breaking stuff and dead interesting.

This is cheesier than all the mousetraps in a Cheddar factory.

Limerick

You may feel relieved to survive
All disasters out there – may
you thrive!
But you've not escaped yet,
As next-up comes the threat
Of waking up BURIED ALIVE...
Eeeeek!

Did you hear about the woman who was buried alive? It was a disastrously grave mistake.

Have you ever been
tempted to wonder
What it's like to be
buried right under...
Nailed down in a Coffin
Where it's unsafe to blow
off-in,
As you'll choke from a
deadly grave blunder!

A DISASTROUS END –
Buried Alive

NOOOOOOOOO

What's your worst nightmare? For many people, it used to be being buried by mistake and waking up buried underground and unable to escape. That's because such nightmares really did happen. Doctors weren't always accurate when they declared a patient dead, so sometimes someone woke up... when it was too late. That's why some people had alarm bells fitted inside their coffins just in case. Today, such disasters are very rare... as far as we know...

A fate worse than death

When Madam Blunden was declared to be dead in 1896, she was buried in the family vault in Basingstoke, England. The vault was under a boys' school. The day after the funeral, some boys heard a noise from the vault below. The coffin inside was opened just in time to witness Madam Blunden's final breath. Despite attempts to revive her, Madam Blunden didn't survive. In her coffin, she had torn at her face and had broken all her fingernails, presumably in a desperate attempt to escape.

Interesting Fact:

Historical documents from the 17th century show that plague victims often collapsed and seemed to be dead, with many recorded cases of people with plague being buried alive.

Can you believe it?

Many 'safety coffins' were invented during the 18th and 19th centuries. A safety coffin was fitted with a mechanism to allow the occupant to signal that he or she has been buried alive.

The Bateson Life Revival Device was an iron bell mounted in a small bell-tower on the lid of the casket, the bell rope attached to the hands of the body through a hole in the coffin lid. Bateson's Belfry was invented in 1852 – and George Bateson was even awarded a medal by Queen Victoria for his services to the dead.

Interesting Fact:

The fear of being buried alive is called taphephobia.
The word 'taphephobia' comes from the Greek 'taphos' meaning 'grave' – 'phobia' from the Greek 'phobos' meaning 'fear'. Probably most of us have just a little taphephobia!

Newspaper report from 1877

(British Medical Journal)

8th December, 1877. It appeared from the evidence that a woman was buried, believed to be dead, while she was only in a trance. Some days afterwards, the grave in which she had been placed was opened to receive another body. It was found that the clothes which covered the unfortunate woman were torn to pieces. The Court, after hearing the case, sentenced the doctor who had signed the death certificate, and the mayor who had authorized the burial, each to three months' imprisonment.

From misfortune to miracle

In 1915, 30-year-old Essie Dunbar of South Carolina, USA, suffered from a fit and died – or so everyone thought. After declaring her dead, doctors placed Essie's body in a coffin and fixed her funeral for late the next day so that her sister from far away could attend.

However, Essie's sister was delayed and she arrived to see the last clods of dirt thrown onto the grave. She insisted on seeing Essie one last time so ordered that the body be removed. When the coffin lid was opened, Essie sat up and smiled at all around her. She lived for another 47 years. Disaster cancelled.

Dead lucky

19-year-old Frenchman
Angelo Hays was speeding on
his motorbike in 1937 when
he crashed and was thrown
headfirst into a brick wall. Hays'
face was so disfigured that his
parents weren't allowed to view
the body. Finding no pulse, doctors
declared Hays dead.

It was a family disaster and three days later, Angelo was buried. But because his father had recently taken out life insurance on his son, the insurance company insisted on digging up the body as they suspected Angelo had been murdered.

To everyone's surprise, when the coffin was opened, Angelo's body was still warm. After being rushed to intensive care, Angelo made a full recovery. In fact, he became a French celebrity.

It's not the cough that'll carry you off. It's the coffin they'll carry you off in.

In the 1970s he went on tour in a souped-up coffin he invented with cushions, a food locker, toilet, and even a library. This time he was prepared!

MORE
bungles and
blunders
oops

Englishman Bobby Leach was known for his daredevil antics. In 1911, his most famous death-defying stunt was surviving going over the Niagara Falls in a barrel. The fall fractured his jaw and broke both knee-caps, but it didn't kill him.

He was something of a hero but on one of his publicity tours in New Zealand, he walked down the street and slipped on a banana skin (some say an orange peel - but it's a fruitless debate). He broke his leg which became infected with gangrene, and was eventually amputated. He died from complications following the operation.

So, the man who survived a huge drop over Niagara Falls (along with many other very dangerous stunts) was finally brought down by squashed fruit.

I've no idea where I am.

In case you were wondering, Annie Edson Taylor was the first person to survive a trip over Niagara Falls in a barrel (in 1901 on her 63rd birthday). This American schoolteacher emerged very dazed and lived for almost 20 more years.

The next daredevil in a barrel to try Niagara Falls was another Englishman, Charles Stephens. When his heavy oak barrel hit the water after the drop over the Falls in 1920, Stephens crashed out of the bottom. He was killed and only one arm was ever recovered.

A Walking Disaster

At the age of 63 in 2010, Douglas McCorquodale was named Scotland's most accident-prone man. He once had to get an eye-patch after spray-painting himself in the face - then fell in a hole and broke his arm as he left hospital.

That looks like a right barrel of laughs.

HIS OTHER
DISASTERS INCLUDE:

1. Falling out the back of his van and knocking himself unconscious

2. Smothering himself with cooking oil instead of sun cream on an Italian beach.

3. Falling through a frozen pond.

4. Building a wonky worktop which collapsed, scalding him with a kettle of boiling water

He said, 'It's not just me I've damaged. I once put a screwdriver in my back pocket, sat down and tore our new leather settee. I jumped up and dropped a cigarette, burning the carpet. I've been banned from using tools around the house and DIY is now out of the question.'

Surely It Couldn't Get Worse

It's been one of those days today...
Disastrous right from the start,
An accident-prone catastrophe-zone;
You name it, and it fell apart.
I leapt out of bed just as soon as I'd woken,
Stubbed my foot on the teapot and was rather outspoken
For the best china tea set and three toes got broken...

SURELY IT COULDN'T GET WORSE!

It's been one of those days today...
Calamities round every corner;
A mass of mishaps made the greenhouse collapse
On my Grandma – with no time to warn her.
So I did quick repairs at the drop of a hat
And the drop of a hammer and spanner, at that.
At last it stood firm... till a sneeze from the cat...

SURELY IT COULDN'T
GET WORSE!
(But it did)

CRASH

It's been one of those days today...
The wall needed plaster and paint,
So I thought I would try my unique D.I.Y.
But it caused quite a lot of complaint.
Aunt Mildred was coming – I had to paint faster,
But my ladder dislodged half a ton of wet plaster
That fell on dear auntie – oh what a disaster!

SURELY IT COULDN'T GET WORSE!
(But it did)

It's been one of those days today...
I tried to help out in the garden
With thoughtful intent, I laid some cement
But nothing would make the stuff harden.
So now my new path is a syrupy failure,
Repairing it's such a HUGE paraphernalia
So I'm leaving it all and I'm off to Australia...

WHERE AT LEAST IT CAN'T GET ANY WORSE!
(But it did)

What a RATastrophic disaster.

Finally...

This is Captain Roger speaking. On behalf of my crew. I'd like to welcome you aboard Overseas Airways flight 602 from New York to London. We are currently flying at a height of 35,000 feet midway across the Atlantic.

I'm itching to know what happens next.

'If you look out of the windows on the starboard side of the aircraft, you will observe that both the starboard engines are on fire. The inflight movie will be 'Air Disaster 2' and begins in a few minutes. If you look out of the windows on the port side, you will observe that the port wing has fallen off.

If you look down towards the Atlantic Ocean, you will see a little yellow life raft with three people in it waving at you. That's me your captain, the co-pilot, and one of the air stewards. This is a recorded message. Enjoy your flight. Roger and out!'

Very very finally cheesily

I'm turtley shell-shocked.

Did you hear about the lorry full of tortoises that collided with a van full of terrapins? It was a turtle disaster.

There's been a disastrous crash on the motorway. A lorry load of glue crashed with a lorry full of wigs. You'll be stuck in traffic for ages while police comb the area.

Did you know you can now get Armageddon Cheese? It says on the packet 'Best Before End...'

If you thought that joke was bad but if you survived some of the truly foul facts or other cheesy jokes in this book, take a look at the other wacky titles in this revolting series. They're all guaranteed to make you groan and squirm like never before. You have been warned!

QUIZ

1. In what year did a wooden amphitheatre collapse near Rome?

a) 40 AD

b) 27 AD

c) 1987 AD

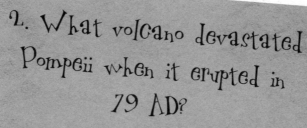

2. What volcano devastated Pompeii when it erupted in 79 AD?

a) Vesuvius

b) Mount Etna

c) Mount Doom

3. What percentage of the population of Europe were killed by the Black Death between 1347 and 1350?

a) 33 percent

b) 60 percent

c) 100 percent

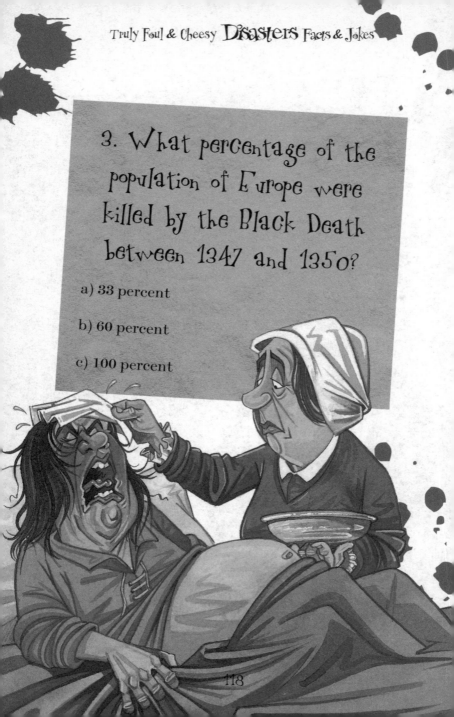

4. What is the fear of being buried alive?

a) Taurophobia

b) Technophobia

c) Taphephobia

I'm not in fancy dress - I always look like this.

5. Which king nearly went up in flames at a fancy dress ball?

a) Charles VI of France

b) Henry VIII of England

c) Elvis Presley

6. In what year did the Titanic sink?

a) 1900

b) 1912

c) 1870

It's unthinkable this ship is sinkable.

7. What is underneath Yellowstone National Park?

a) Buried treasure

b) A supervolcano

c) A ticking bomb

8. Where did giant hailstones fall in 1986?

a) Bangladesh

b) Liverpool

c) New York

9. What is smog?

a) A smelly cat

b) A cleaning product

c) A mix of dense fog and deadly fumes

I fear this is the end of me and the book

10. What did a Queensland shopkeeper hide from during the Australian floods of 2011?

a) A bull shark

b) Jellyfish

c) A surfboarding kangaroo

Answers:

1 = b
2 = a
3 = a
4 = c
5 = a
6 = b
7 = b
8 = a
9 = c
10 = a

GLOSSARY

Amphitheatre: an open-roofed, circular building with an empty space in the centre where shows and entertainment can be staged.

Atomic bombs: bombs that use the energy released by the splitting of radioactive materials to create enormous explosions.

Cyclone: also called a hurricane. A circular storm in tropical oceans characterised by high winds, heavy rain and low atmospheric pressure.

Earth's crust: the top layer of rock covering the planet.

Frostbite: when living tissue, such as skin, freezes in very cold temperatures, causing damage to the cells.

Meteor: Small planet-shaped bodies of ice and rock that orbit our solar system and sometimes collide with the Earth.

Niagara Falls: A very large waterfall on the border between the state of New York and Ontario, Canada.

INDEX

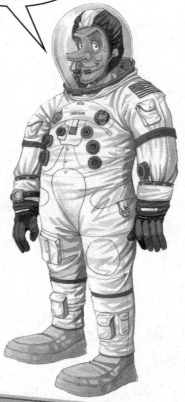

I finished reading this Truly
Foul & Cheesy book on:

........../........../..........